I Get It! Times Tables

The WORKBOOK

WITH TONNES OF EXAMPLES AND MORE TIMES TABLE TRICKS

by Larissa Bjornson

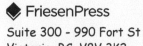 FriesenPress

Suite 300 - 990 Fort St
Victoria, BC, V8V 3K2
Canada

www.friesenpress.com

ISBN
978-1-03-911057-1 (Hardcover)
978-1-03-911056-4 (Paperback)
978-1-03-911058-8 (eBook)

1. Juvenile Nonfiction, Mathematics, Arithmetic

Distributed to the trade by The Ingram Book Company

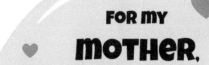

TABLE OF CONTENTS

MULTIPLICATION

MULTIPLICATION is a fast way to add groups together that are the same size. In multiplication, we say, "multiplied by," or "times." The sign we use for multiplication is the symbol x.

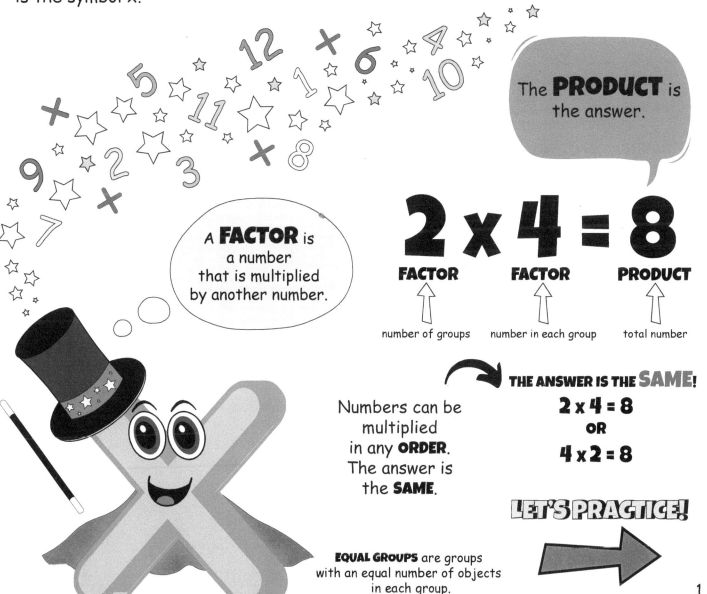

The **PRODUCT** is the answer.

A **FACTOR** is a number that is multiplied by another number.

$$2 \times 4 = 8$$

FACTOR	FACTOR	PRODUCT
number of groups	number in each group	total number

Numbers can be multiplied in any **ORDER**. The answer is the **SAME**.

THE ANSWER IS THE **SAME**!

2 x 4 = 8
OR
4 x 2 = 8

LET'S PRACTICE!

EQUAL GROUPS are groups with an equal number of objects in each group.

1

ONE TIMES TABLE
Skater Park Tricks

Check out Sam the skateboarder's cool math trick for solving the one times table.

That Number!

IT'S JUST THAT NUMBER!

1 x 5 = 5

It's just that number!

IT'S JUST THAT NUMBER!

1 x 8 = 8

It's just that number!

1 x 1 = 1
1 x 2 = 2
1 x 3 = 3
1 x 4 = 4
1 x 5 = 5
1 x 6 = 6
1 x 7 = 7
1 x 8 = 8
1 x 9 = 9
1 x 10 = 10
1 x 11 = 11
1 x 12 = 12

Multiplying any number by 1 means you end up with the same number at the end of the question.

ONE TIMES TABLE
Practice

Work out these multiplication questions.
Fill in your answer on the skateboard ramp.

EXAMPLE 1:
1 x 2 = 2
It's just that number!

EXAMPLE 2:
1 x 10 = 10
It's just that number!

1 x 5 =

1 x 9 =

1 x 3 =

1 x 1 =

1 x 8 =

1 x 6 =

TWO TIMES TABLE
Double the Fun

Take a walk with Ivy and her dog Rover,
and discover how to use doubles to solve the two times table.

DOUBLE IT!
$2 \times 3 = 6$
Double it ⟹ 3 + 3 = 6

DOUBLE IT!
$2 \times 9 = 18$
Double it ⟹ 9 + 9 = 18

When you
multiply two by any number,
you just
DOUBLE that number.

DOUBLE IT!

$2 \times 1 = 2$
$2 \times 2 = 4$
$2 \times 3 = 6$
$2 \times 4 = 8$
$2 \times 5 = 10$
$2 \times 6 = 12$
$2 \times 7 = 14$
$2 \times 8 = 16$
$2 \times 9 = 18$
$2 \times 10 = 20$
$2 \times 11 = 22$
$2 \times 12 = 24$

A **DOUBLE**
is the
same number
added to itself.

2x DOUBLE IT!

TWO TIMES TABLE
practice

Complete these multiplication questions.
Write your answer in the center of the flower.

EXAMPLE 1:
2 x 4 = 8
DOUBLE IT!
Double 4 that makes 8.

EXAMPLE 2:
2 x 7 = 14
DOUBLE IT!
Double 7 that makes 14.

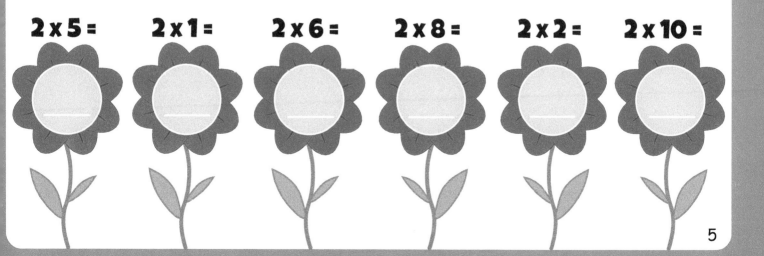

2 x 5 =   2 x 1 =   2 x 6 =   2 x 8 =   2 x 2 =   2 x 10 =

5

HOME   GUEST

3 x 2 = ☐ : 3 x 4 = ☐

THREE TIMES TABLE
HAT TRICK

A hat trick occurs when a player scores
THREE goals in **ONE** game.

Ice-skate with Duke and learn a fun trick for solving the three times table.

STEP 1:
Draw a table.

STEP 2:
Write this pattern.

STEP 3:
Next, write this pattern.

Write the number **ZERO** →
across the top row.

Write the number **ONE** →
across the middle row.

Write the number **TWO** →
across the bottom row.

0	0	0
1	1	1
2	2	2

03	06	09
12	15	18
21	24	27

↑   ↑   ↑

Start from the bottom and count up from 1-9. When you get to the top of one column, go back to the bottom of the next column and keep on counting!

3x1	3x2	3x3
03	06	09
3x4	3x5	3x6
12	15	18
3x7	3x8	3x9
21	24	27

TAKE A LOOK ←

ROWS - go side to side
COLUMNS - go up and down

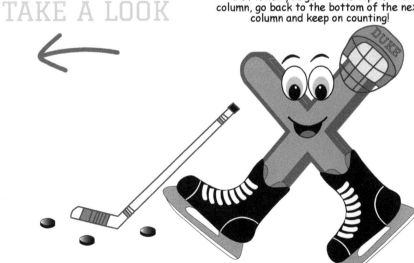

3x HOME GUEST DOUBLE IT, AND ADD A GROUP!

THREE TIMES TABLE
PRACTICE

Solve each of the multiplication questions. Fill in your answer inside the hockey nets.

EXAMPLE 1:
$3 \times 5 = 15$

Double it, and add a group!

Double 5 that makes 10.
Add a group of 5 and you get 15!

EXAMPLE 2:
$3 \times 7 = 21$

Double it, and add a group!

Double 7 that makes 14.
Add a group of 7 and you get 21!

3 x 5 =

3 x 8 =

3 x 4 =

3 x 9 =

3 x 6 =

3 x 2 =

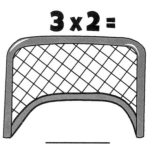

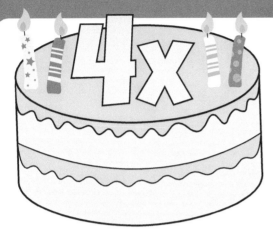

FOUR TIMES TABLE
COOKIE'S
DOUBLE IT
DOUBLE IT AGAIN
BAKESHOP

Follow Cookie's amazing recipe for solving the four times table.

**DOUBLE IT,
DOUBLE IT AGAIN!**

$$4 \times 3 = 12$$
Double it ⟹ 3 + 3 = 6
Double it again ⟹ 6 + 6 = 12

**DOUBLE IT,
DOUBLE IT AGAIN!**

$$4 \times 6 = 24$$
Double it ⟹ 6 + 6 = 12
Double it again ⟹ 12 + 12 = 24

Double it,
double it again!

The four times table
is **DOUBLE** the
two times table.

All of your answers
in the four times table
are **EVEN NUMBERS**!

$4 \times 1 = 4$
$4 \times 2 = 8$
$4 \times 3 = 12$
$4 \times 4 = 16$
$4 \times 5 = 20$
$4 \times 6 = 24$
$4 \times 7 = 28$
$4 \times 8 = 32$
$4 \times 9 = 36$
$4 \times 10 = 40$
$4 \times 11 = 44$
$4 \times 12 = 48$

8

FOUR TIMES TABLE
Practice

Work out these multiplication questions.
Fill in your answer on Cookie's bakers' hat.

EXAMPLE 1:
4 x 2 = 8
Double it, double it again!
Double 2 that makes 4.
Double 4 and you get 8!

EXAMPLE 2:
4 x 5 = 20
Double it, double it again!
Double 5 that makes 10.
Double 10 and you get 20!

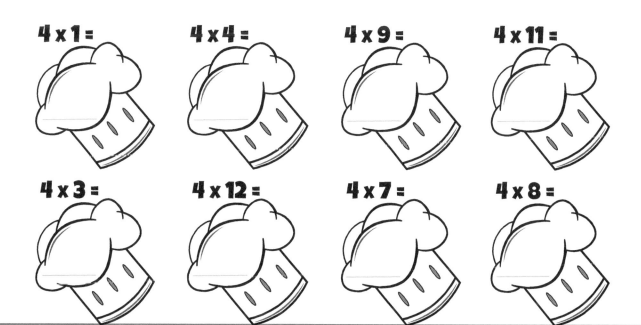

4 x 1 =

4 x 4 =

4 x 9 =

4 x 11 =

4 x 3 =

4 x 12 =

4 x 7 =

4 x 8 =

9

FIVE TIMES TABLE
ONE, TWO,
THREE , FOUR , FIVE

Follow Rocky's lead and learn an awesome trick for solving the five times table.

SKIP COUNT BY FIVES!
5 x 3 = 15
Count by fives
5, 10, 15
You 've got it!

0, 5, 10, 15, 20, 25, 30, 35, 40, 45, 50, 55, 60 ...

SKIP COUNT BY FIVES!
5 x 6 = 30
Count by fives
5, 10, 15, 20, 25, 30

0, 5, 10, 15, 20, 25, 30, 35, 40, 45, 50, 55, 60 ...

When you multiply by five, your answer will always end in **FIVE** or **ZERO**.

FIVE TIMES TABLE
PRACTICE

5x

SKIP COUNT BY FIVES!

Find the product.
Write your answer on top of the speaker.
Remember, the product is the answer.

EXAMPLE 1:
$$5 \times 4 = 20$$
Skip count by fives!
5, 10, 15, 20

EXAMPLE 2:
$$5 \times 7 = 35$$
Skip count by fives!
5, 10, 15, 20, 25, 30, 35

5 x 2 = _____   5 x 5 = _____

5 x 1 = _____   5 x 11 = _____

5 x 10 = _____   5 x 3 = _____

5 x 6 = _____   5 x 12 = _____

6 x 2 = ?   6 x 9 = ?

SIX TIMES TABLE
Math Experiment

Join Sophie's math experiment and discover new tricks for solving the six times table.

If you multiply six by an even number, it will end in the **SAME DIGIT**.

You can find the other numbers in the six times table by **ADDING** six to the previous number.

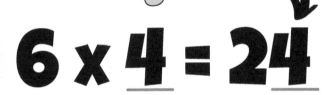

6 x 4 = 24

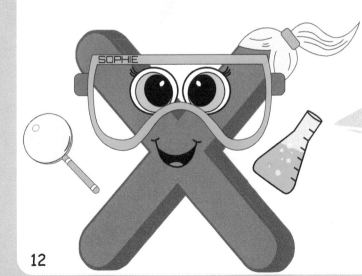

When multiplying the number **6** by **2**, **4**, **6**, or **8** the number in the tens place will be half the number in the ones place.

This **ONLY** works when multiplying the number six by 2, 4, 6, or 8.

6 x 1 = 6
6 x 2 = 12
6 x 3 = 18
6 x 4 = 24
6 x 5 = 30
6 x 6 = 36
6 x 7 = 42
6 x 8 = 48
6 x 9 = 54
6 x 10 = 60
6 x 11 = 66
6 x 12 = 72

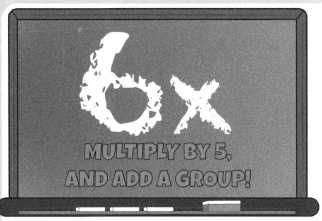

SIX TIMES TABLE
Practice

Solve each of the multiplication questions.
Write your answer inside Sophie's safety glasses.

EXAMPLE 1:
6 x 3 = 18
Multiply by 5, and add a group!
3 times 5 that makes 15.
Add a group of 3 and you get 18!

EXAMPLE 2:
6 x 8 = 48
Multiply by 5, and add a group!
8 times 5 that makes 40.
Add a group of 8 and you get 48!

6 x 10 = **6 x 5 =** **6 x 11 =**

6 x 6 = **6 x 12 =** **6 x 1 =**

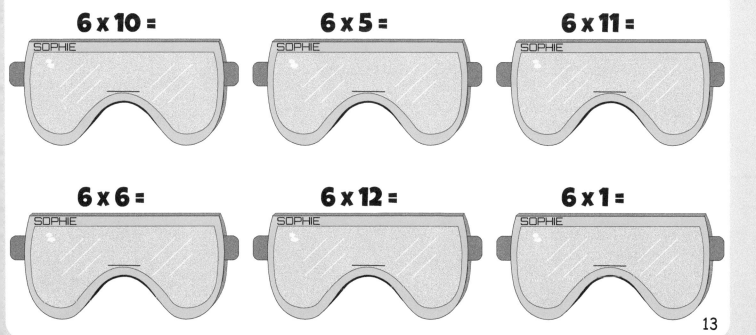

SEVEN TIMES TABLE
Let's Make a Picture

Draw a picture with Pistachio the painter and learn a fun trick to solve the seven times table.

STEP 1:
Draw a table.

STEP 2:
Write the numbers 1-9, starting in the upper right corner and descending.

7	4	①	←**START HERE**
8	5	2
9	6	3

STEP 3:
Write this number pattern starting with 0.

MOVE ACROSS EACH ROW

START HERE →	⓪	1	2
REPEAT THE NUMBER 2 →	②	3	4
REPEAT THE NUMBER 4 →	④	5	6

STEP 4:
Put step 2 and step 3 together.

Now, we can read the 7 x 1 to 7 x 9 times table from left to right!

7x1	7x2	7x3
07	14	21
7x4	**7x5**	**7x6**
28	35	42
7x7	**7x8**	**7x9**
49	56	63

SEVEN TIMES TABLE
Practice

Work out these multiplication questions.
Fill in your answer on the painting canvas.

EXAMPLE 1:
7 x 2 = 14

Multiply by 5, and add a double!
2 times 5 that makes 10.
Double 2 that makes 4.
Add them together 10 + 4.
And you get 14!

EXAMPLE 2:
7 x 4 = 28

Multiply by 5, and add a double!
4 times 5 that makes 20.
Double 4 that makes 8.
Add them together 20 + 8.
And you get 28!

7 x 3 =

7 x 8 =

7 x 6 =

7 x 1 =

EIGHT TIMES TABLE
MATH WORK AHEAD

Join Corey the carpenter's construction crew and see how to solve the eight times table.

ALL THE MULTIPLES OF 8 ARE EVEN!

DOUBLE IT, DOUBLE IT AGAIN, DOUBLE IT AGAIN!

$8 \times 2 = 16$

Double it ⟹ 2 + 2 = 4
Double it again ⟹ 4 + 4 = 8
Double it again ⟹ 8 + 8 = 16

DOUBLE IT, DOUBLE IT AGAIN, DOUBLE IT AGAIN!

$8 \times 5 = 40$

Double it ⟹ 5 + 5 = 10
Double it again ⟹ 10 + 10 = 20
Double it again ⟹ 20 + 20 = 40

DOUBLE, DOUBLE, DOUBLE!

Double, Double, Double!

Multiples of **8** follow a pattern of **8, 6, 4, 2,** and **0** in the ones place.

A multiple is the number you get after multiplying a number by another number.

UNDER CONSTRUCTION

$8 \times 1 = 8$
$8 \times 2 = 16$
$8 \times 3 = 24$
$8 \times 4 = 32$
$8 \times 5 = 40$
$8 \times 6 = 48$
$8 \times 7 = 56$
$8 \times 8 = 64$
$8 \times 9 = 72$
$8 \times 10 = 80$
$8 \times 11 = 88$
$8 \times 12 = 96$

EIGHT TIMES TABLE
MATH
WORK
AHEAD

Complete these multiplication questions.
Write your answer on the hard hat.

EXAMPLE 1:

8 x 4 = 32

Double, double, double!
Double 4 that makes 8.
Double 8 that makes 16.
Double 16 and you get 32!

EXAMPLE 2:

8 x 6 = 48

Double, double, double!
Double 6 that makes 12.
Double 12 that makes 24.
Double 24 and you get 48!

8 x 3 =

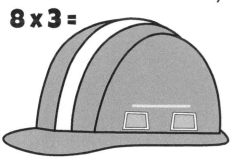

8 x 9 =

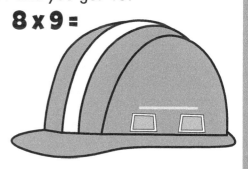

UNDER CONSTRUCTION

8 x 1 =

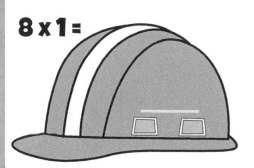

8 x 11 =

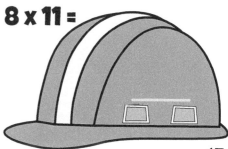

9x NINE TIMES TABLE
Counting Challenge

Join Astronaut Annie's math mission
and discover an out-of-this-world nine times table trick.

Check it out

STEP 1:
Write the numbers
0 to **9**
in a downward direction.

STEP 2:
Write the numbers
0 to **9**
in an upward direction.

0 9	9 x 1 = 09
1 8	9 x 2 = 18
2 7	9 x 3 = 27
3 6	9 x 4 = 36
4 5	9 x 5 = 45
5 4	9 x 6 = 54
6 3	9 x 7 = 63
7 2	9 x 8 = 72
8 1	9 x 9 = 81
9 0	9 x 10 = 90

NINE TIMES TABLE
Practice

Work out these multiplication facts.
Write your answer inside the rocket.

EXAMPLE 1:

9 x 2 = 18

Multiply by 10, and subtract a group!
2 times 10 that makes 20.
Subtract a group of 2.
And you get 18!

EXAMPLE 2:

9 x 5 = 45

Multiply by 10, and subtract a group!
5 times 10 that makes 50.
Subtract a group of 5.
And you get 45!

9 x 4 =

9 x 7 =

9 x 9 =

9 x 6 =

9 x 3 =

10x

Just Add a Zero!

Come and visit Flynn's farm
and see how to solve the ten times table.

ADD A ZERO!

10 x 4 = ?
10 x 4 = 40

Add a zero.
You get 40!

ADD A ZERO!

10 x 9 = ?
10 x 9 = 90

Add a zero.
You get 90!

Take the number
you are multiplying by
and put a ZERO right after it.

All of your
answers will end in
ZERO.

Add
a
zero!

The ten times table is made
by skip counting by ten!

FARMERS' MARKET

10 x 1 = 10
10 x 2 = 20
10 x 3 = 30
10 x 4 = 40
10 x 5 = 50
10 x 6 = 60
10 x 7 = 70
10 x 8 = 80
10 x 9 = 90
10 x 10 = 100
10 x 11 = 110
10 x 12 = 120

10x
JUST ADD A ZERO!

TEN TIMES TABLE
Practice

The product is the answer.

Find the product.
Write your answer on the tractor.

EXAMPLE 1:

10 x 3 = 30

Add a zero.
You get 30!

EXAMPLE 2:

10 x 8 = 80

Add a zero.
You get 80!

10 x 2 = ___

10 x 5 = ___

10 x 11 = ___

10 x 1 = ___

10 x 7 = ___

10 x 10 = ___

21

ELEVEN TIMES TABLE
SEEING DOUBLE

Visit Doc's clinic and learn fun tricks to solve the eleven times table.

11x
- ✓ 11 x 3 = 33
- ✓ 11 x 5 = 55
- ✓ 11 x 7 = 77

When you multiply **11 x 1** to **11 x 9** the ones and tens digit will be the same.

To multiply any two digit number by **11**: **ADD** the digits of your number together then put the **SUM** of these digits between the two digits of your number.

11 X 12 = 132

Your number is **12**.
ADD the digits of your number together **1 + 2 = 3**.
Now, put the **SUM** between the two digits of your number **132**.

SEEING DOUBLE!
11 X 4 = 44

THIS WORKS FOR ANY TWO DIGIT NUMBER IF THE SUM OF THE TWO DIGITS IS 9 OR LESS.

For numbers where the sum of the digits is larger than nine

CARRY THE ONE OVER TO THE NEXT DIGIT.

22

11x
MULTIPLY BY 10, AND ADD A GROUP!

ELEVEN TIMES TABLE
PRACTICE

YOU CAN MULTIPLY BY TEN AND ADD A GROUP TOO!

Complete these multiplication questions.
Write your answer on Doc's medical case.

EXAMPLE 1:
11 x 6 = 66
Multiply by 10, and add a group!
6 times 10 that makes 60.
Add a group of 6 and you get 66!

EXAMPLE 2:
11 x 9 = 99
Multiply by 10, and add a group!
9 times 10 that makes 90.
Add a group of 9 and you get 99!

11 x 1 =

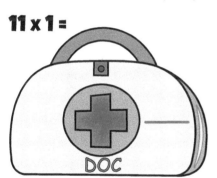

11 x 4 =

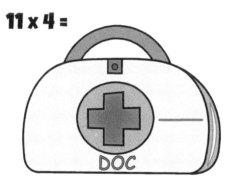

11 x 12 =

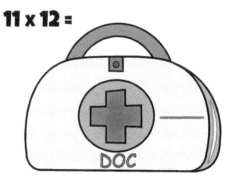

11 x 2 =

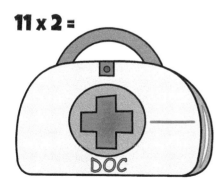

11 x 11 =

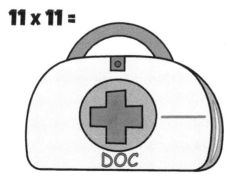

11 x 10 =

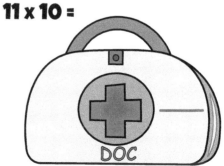

23

TWELVE TIMES TABLE
DANCE SCHOOL TRICKS

Join Daphne's dance school
and find out how to solve the twelve times table.

MULTIPLY BY 10, AND ADD A DOUBLE!

12 x 3 = 36

Multiply by 10 ⟹ 3 × 10 = 30
Double 3 ⟹ 3 + 3 = 6
Add them together ⟹ 30 + 6 = 36

MULTIPLY BY 10, AND ADD A DOUBLE!

12 x 5 = 60

Multiply by 10 ⟹ 5 × 10 = 50
Double 5 ⟹ 5 + 5 = 10
Add them together ⟹ 50 + 10 = 60

The twelve times table has a repeating pattern in the **ONES** place.

Look at how the numbers in the ones place repeat all throughout the 12x table.

12 x 1 = 12
12 x 2 = 24
12 x 3 = 36
12 x 4 = 48
12 x 5 = 60
12 x 6 = 72
12 x 7 = 84
12 x 8 = 96
12 x 9 = 108
12 x 10 = 120
12 x 11 = 132
12 x 12 = 144

24

TWELVE TIMES TABLE
PRACTICE

12x
MULTIPLY BY 10, AND ADD A DOUBLE!

Work out these multiplication questions.
Write your answer in the stage light.

EXAMPLE 1:
$12 \times 2 = 24$

Multiply by 10, and add a double!
2 times 10 that makes 20.
Double 2 that makes 4.
Add them together 20 + 4.
And you get 24!

EXAMPLE 2:
$12 \times 9 = 108$

Multiply by 10, and add a double!
9 times 10 that makes 90.
Double 9 that makes 18.
Add them together 90 + 18.
And you get 108!

$12 \times 4 =$ _____

$12 \times 1 =$ _____

$12 \times 7 =$ _____

$12 \times 6 =$ _____

$12 \times 11 =$ _____

MULTIPLY BY 10, AND ADD A DOUBLE!

THE TIMES TABLE TEAM

YOU CAN GET IT!

7x
MULTIPLY BY 5, AND ADD A DOUBLE!

8x
DOUBLE, DOUBLE, DOUBLE!

9x
MULTIPLY BY 10, AND SUBTRACT A GROUP!

10x
JUST ADD A ZERO!

11x
MULTIPLY BY 10, AND ADD A GROUP!

12x
MULTIPLY BY 10, AND ADD A DOUBLE!

MULTIPLICATION TABLE

A MULTIPLICATION TABLE SHOWS YOU ALL THE ANSWERS TO THE TIMES TABLES!

To use the
MULTIPLICATION TABLE
just follow
the steps.

STEP 1 ⟹ Track your finger down the yellow column of numbers on the left side of the table until you find the first number in a question.

STEP 2 ⟹ Now, track a different finger along the blue row of numbers at the top of the table until it matches the second number in a question.

STEP 3 ⟹ Finally, run your first finger across the table and your second finger down the table. The number where your fingers meet is your answer.

X	1	2	3	4	5	6	7	8	9	10	11	12
1	1	2	3	4	5	6	7	8	9	10	11	12
2	2	4	6	8	10	12	14	16	18	20	22	24
3	3	6	9	12	15	18	21	24	27	30	33	36
4	4	8	12	16	20	24	28	32	36	40	44	48
5	5	10	15	20	25	30	35	40	45	50	55	60
6	6	12	18	24	30	36	42	48	54	60	66	72
7	7	14	21	28	35	42	49	56	63	70	77	84
8	8	16	24	32	40	48	56	64	72	80	88	96
9	9	18	27	36	45	54	63	72	81	90	99	108
10	10	20	30	40	50	60	70	80	90	100	110	120
11	11	22	33	44	55	66	77	88	99	110	121	132
12	12	24	36	48	60	72	84	96	108	120	132	144

YOUR MULTIPLICATION TABLES

THIS IS WHERE YOU CAN FIND ALL OF THE ANSWERS!

1x
1 x 1 = 1
1 x 2 = 2
1 x 3 = 3
1 x 4 = 4
1 x 5 = 5
1 x 6 = 6
1 x 7 = 7
1 x 8 = 8
1 x 9 = 9
1 x 10 = 10
1 x 11 = 11
1 x 12 = 12

2x
2 x 1 = 2
2 x 2 = 4
2 x 3 = 6
2 x 4 = 8
2 x 5 = 10
2 x 6 = 12
2 x 7 = 14
2 x 8 = 16
2 x 9 = 18
2 x 10 = 20
2 x 11 = 22
2 x 12 = 24

3x
3 x 1 = 3
3 x 2 = 6
3 x 3 = 9
3 x 4 = 12
3 x 5 = 15
3 x 6 = 18
3 x 7 = 21
3 x 8 = 24
3 x 9 = 27
3 x 10 = 30
3 x 11 = 33
3 x 12 = 36

4x
4 x 1 = 4
4 x 2 = 8
4 x 3 = 12
4 x 4 = 16
4 x 5 = 20
4 x 6 = 24
4 x 7 = 28
4 x 8 = 32
4 x 9 = 36
4 x 10 = 40
4 x 11 = 44
4 x 12 = 48

5x
5 x 1 = 5
5 x 2 = 10
5 x 3 = 15
5 x 4 = 20
5 x 5 = 25
5 x 6 = 30
5 x 7 = 35
5 x 8 = 40
5 x 9 = 45
5 x 10 = 50
5 x 11 = 55
5 x 12 = 60

6x
6 x 1 = 6
6 x 2 = 12
6 x 3 = 18
6 x 4 = 24
6 x 5 = 30
6 x 6 = 36
6 x 7 = 42
6 x 8 = 48
6 x 9 = 54
6 x 10 = 60
6 x 11 = 66
6 x 12 = 72

7x
7 x 1 = 7
7 x 2 = 14
7 x 3 = 21
7 x 4 = 28
7 x 5 = 35
7 x 6 = 42
7 x 7 = 49
7 x 8 = 56
7 x 9 = 63
7 x 10 = 70
7 x 11 = 77
7 x 12 = 84

8x
8 x 1 = 8
8 x 2 = 16
8 x 3 = 24
8 x 4 = 32
8 x 5 = 40
8 x 6 = 48
8 x 7 = 56
8 x 8 = 64
8 x 9 = 72
8 x 10 = 80
8 x 11 = 88
8 x 12 = 96

9x
9 x 1 = 9
9 x 2 = 18
9 x 3 = 27
9 x 4 = 36
9 x 5 = 45
9 x 6 = 54
9 x 7 = 63
9 x 8 = 72
9 x 9 = 81
9 x 10 = 90
9 x 11 = 99
9 x 12 = 108

10x
10 x 1 = 10
10 x 2 = 20
10 x 3 = 30
10 x 4 = 40
10 x 5 = 50
10 x 6 = 60
10 x 7 = 70
10 x 8 = 80
10 x 9 = 90
10 x 10 = 100
10 x 11 = 110
10 x 12 = 120

11x
11 x 1 = 11
11 x 2 = 22
11 x 3 = 33
11 x 4 = 44
11 x 5 = 55
11 x 6 = 66
11 x 7 = 77
11 x 8 = 88
11 x 9 = 99
11 x 10 = 110
11 x 11 = 121
11 x 12 = 132

12x
12 x 1 = 12
12 x 2 = 24
12 x 3 = 36
12 x 4 = 48
12 x 5 = 60
12 x 6 = 72
12 x 7 = 84
12 x 8 = 96
12 x 9 = 108
12 x 10 = 120
12 x 11 = 132
12 x 12 = 144

ONE TIMES PRACTICE

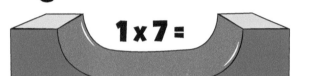
1 x 7 =

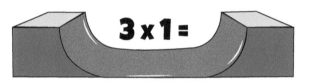
3 x 1 =

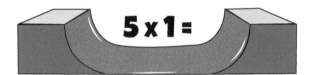
5 x 1 =

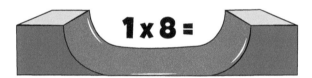
1 x 8 =

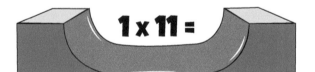
1 x 11 =

6 x 1 =

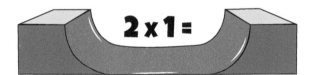
2 x 1 =

1 x 1 =

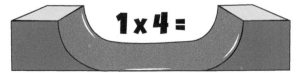
1 x 4 =

10 x 1 =

MORE PRACTICE...

1 x 3 = __   7 x 1 = __   1 x 9 = __

5 x 1 = __   1 x 6 = __   12 x 1 = __

1 x 1 = __   2 x 1 = __   1 x 4 = __

10 x 1 = __   1 x 8 = __   11 x 1 = __

$$
\begin{array}{r} 1 \\ \times\ 7 \\ \hline \end{array}
\qquad
\begin{array}{r} 1 \\ \times\ 3 \\ \hline \end{array}
\qquad
\begin{array}{r} 9 \\ \times\ 1 \\ \hline \end{array}
\qquad
\begin{array}{r} 6 \\ \times\ 1 \\ \hline \end{array}
\qquad
\begin{array}{r} 1 \\ \times\ 2 \\ \hline \end{array}
\qquad
\begin{array}{r} 1 \\ \times\ 4 \\ \hline \end{array}
$$

$$
\begin{array}{r} 11 \\ \times\ 1 \\ \hline \end{array}
\qquad
\begin{array}{r} 1 \\ \times\ 5 \\ \hline \end{array}
\qquad
\begin{array}{r} 8 \\ \times\ 1 \\ \hline \end{array}
\qquad
\begin{array}{r} 12 \\ \times\ 1 \\ \hline \end{array}
\qquad
\begin{array}{r} 1 \\ \times\ 1 \\ \hline \end{array}
\qquad
\begin{array}{r} 10 \\ \times\ 1 \\ \hline \end{array}
$$

$$
\begin{array}{r} 5 \\ \times\ 1 \\ \hline \end{array}
\qquad
\begin{array}{r} 3 \\ \times\ 1 \\ \hline \end{array}
\qquad
\begin{array}{r} 1 \\ \times\ 7 \\ \hline \end{array}
\qquad
\begin{array}{r} 1 \\ \times\ 6 \\ \hline \end{array}
\qquad
\begin{array}{r} 8 \\ \times\ 1 \\ \hline \end{array}
\qquad
\begin{array}{r} 2 \\ \times\ 1 \\ \hline \end{array}
$$

2x TWO TIMES PRACTICE

2 x 7 =

1 x 2 =

5 x 2 =

8 x 2 =

2 x 6 =

10 x 2 =

2 x 3 =

2 x 11 =

2 x 4 =

12 x 2 =

MORE PRACTICE...

2 x 8 =___   3 x 2 =___   2 x 4 =___

7 x 2 =___   2 x 6 =___   11 x 2 =___

2 x 2 =___   1 x 2 =___   2 x 5 =___

10 x 2 =___   2 x 9 =___   12 x 2 =___

$$
\begin{array}{cc} 2 \\ \times\ 7 \\ \hline \end{array}
\quad
\begin{array}{cc} 2 \\ \times\ 8 \\ \hline \end{array}
\quad
\begin{array}{cc} 6 \\ \times\ 2 \\ \hline \end{array}
\quad
\begin{array}{cc} 1 \\ \times\ 2 \\ \hline \end{array}
\quad
\begin{array}{cc} 2 \\ \times\ 3 \\ \hline \end{array}
\quad
\begin{array}{cc} 2 \\ \times\ 4 \\ \hline \end{array}
$$

$$
\begin{array}{cc} 11 \\ \times\ 2 \\ \hline \end{array}
\quad
\begin{array}{cc} 2 \\ \times\ 5 \\ \hline \end{array}
\quad
\begin{array}{cc} 3 \\ \times\ 2 \\ \hline \end{array}
\quad
\begin{array}{cc} 12 \\ \times\ 2 \\ \hline \end{array}
\quad
\begin{array}{cc} 2 \\ \times\ 1 \\ \hline \end{array}
\quad
\begin{array}{cc} 10 \\ \times\ 2 \\ \hline \end{array}
$$

$$
\begin{array}{cc} 5 \\ \times\ 2 \\ \hline \end{array}
\quad
\begin{array}{cc} 1 \\ \times\ 2 \\ \hline \end{array}
\quad
\begin{array}{cc} 2 \\ \times\ 7 \\ \hline \end{array}
\quad
\begin{array}{cc} 2 \\ \times\ 6 \\ \hline \end{array}
\quad
\begin{array}{cc} 9 \\ \times\ 2 \\ \hline \end{array}
\quad
\begin{array}{cc} 2 \\ \times\ 2 \\ \hline \end{array}
$$

HOME : GUEST

$3 \times 1 =$ ☐ : $3 \times 9 =$ ☐

THREE TIMES PRACTICE

3 x 2 =

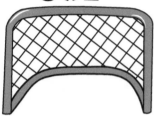

_____

1 x 3 =

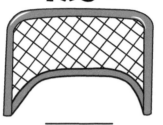

_____

3 x 7 =

_____

3 x 5 =

_____

3 x 6 =

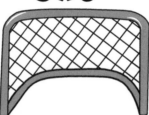

_____

3 x 8 =

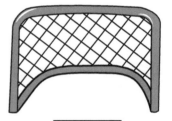

_____

3 x 3 =

_____

11 x 3 =

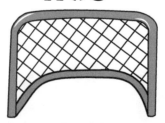

_____

3 x 4 =

_____

MORE PRACTICE...

3 x 8 = ___   3 x 3 = ___   3 x 4 = ___

6 x 3 = ___   3 x 7 = ___   11 x 3 = ___

3 x 2 = ___   1 x 3 = ___   3 x 9 = ___

12 x 3 = ___   3 x 5 = ___   10 x 3 = ___

$$
\begin{array}{r} 3 \\ \times\ 9 \\ \hline \end{array}
\qquad
\begin{array}{r} 3 \\ \times\ 5 \\ \hline \end{array}
\qquad
\begin{array}{r} 2 \\ \times\ 3 \\ \hline \end{array}
\qquad
\begin{array}{r} 1 \\ \times\ 3 \\ \hline \end{array}
\qquad
\begin{array}{r} 3 \\ \times\ 3 \\ \hline \end{array}
\qquad
\begin{array}{r} 3 \\ \times\ 6 \\ \hline \end{array}
$$

$$
\begin{array}{r} 10 \\ \times\ 3 \\ \hline \end{array}
\qquad
\begin{array}{r} 3 \\ \times\ 8 \\ \hline \end{array}
\qquad
\begin{array}{r} 3 \\ \times\ 3 \\ \hline \end{array}
\qquad
\begin{array}{r} 11 \\ \times\ 3 \\ \hline \end{array}
\qquad
\begin{array}{r} 3 \\ \times\ 4 \\ \hline \end{array}
\qquad
\begin{array}{r} 12 \\ \times\ 3 \\ \hline \end{array}
$$

$$
\begin{array}{r} 4 \\ \times\ 3 \\ \hline \end{array}
\qquad
\begin{array}{r} 7 \\ \times\ 3 \\ \hline \end{array}
\qquad
\begin{array}{r} 3 \\ \times\ 8 \\ \hline \end{array}
\qquad
\begin{array}{r} 3 \\ \times\ 9 \\ \hline \end{array}
\qquad
\begin{array}{r} 5 \\ \times\ 3 \\ \hline \end{array}
\qquad
\begin{array}{r} 2 \\ \times\ 3 \\ \hline \end{array}
$$

FOUR TIMES PRACTICE

4 x 2 =

4 x 5 =

4 x 1 =

4 x 8 =

7 x 4 =

9 x 4 =

3 x 4 =

11 x 4 =

4 x 12 =

4 x 4 =

4 x 6 =

4 x 10 =

MORE PRACTICE...

4 x 7 =___   3 x 4 =___   4 x 4 =___

6 x 4 =___   4 x 5 =___   12 x 4 =___

4 x 1 =___   2 x 4 =___   4 x 9 =___

11 x 4 =___   4 x 8 =___   10 x 4 =___

4	4	3	1	4	4
x 8	x 9	x 4	x 4	x 2	x 6

11	4	5	12	4	10
x 4	x 7	x 4	x 4	x 4	x 4

1	8	4	4	5	2
x 4	x 4	x 3	x 9	x 4	x 4

FIVE TIMES PRACTICE

5 x 2 = _____

5 x 4 = _____

5 x 1 = _____

5 x 6 = _____

8 x 5 = _____

9 x 5 = _____

4 x 5 = _____

3 x 5 = _____

MORE PRACTICE...

5 x 6 = __   3 x 5 = __   5 x 2 = __

7 x 5 = __   5 x 5 = __   11 x 5 = __

5 x 4 = __   1 x 5 = __   5 x 8 = __

10 x 5 = __   5 x 9 = __   12 x 5 = __

5	5	3	2	5	5
x 9	x 7	x 5	x 5	x 1	x 6

10	5	5	12	5	11
x 5	x 8	x 5	x 5	x 4	x 5

1	2	5	5	9	4
x 5	x 5	x 3	x 5	x 5	x 5

SIX TIMES PRACTICE

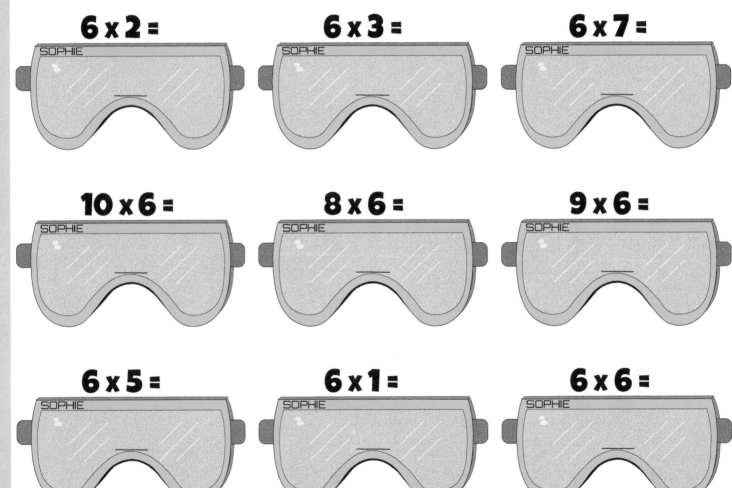

6 x 2 =

6 x 3 =

6 x 7 =

10 x 6 =

8 x 6 =

9 x 6 =

6 x 5 =

6 x 1 =

6 x 6 =

40

MORE PRACTICE...

6 x 2 = ___   4 x 6 = ___   6 x 5 = ___

8 x 6 = ___   6 x 9 = ___   10 x 6 = ___

6 x 1 = ___   3 x 6 = ___   6 x 7 = ___

12 x 6 = ___   6 x 6 = ___   11 x 6 = ___

$$\begin{array}{r} 6 \\ \times\ 8 \\ \hline \end{array} \qquad \begin{array}{r} 6 \\ \times\ 2 \\ \hline \end{array} \qquad \begin{array}{r} 1 \\ \times\ 6 \\ \hline \end{array} \qquad \begin{array}{r} 7 \\ \times\ 6 \\ \hline \end{array} \qquad \begin{array}{r} 6 \\ \times\ 3 \\ \hline \end{array} \qquad \begin{array}{r} 6 \\ \times\ 6 \\ \hline \end{array}$$

$$\begin{array}{r} 12 \\ \times\ 6 \\ \hline \end{array} \qquad \begin{array}{r} 6 \\ \times\ 4 \\ \hline \end{array} \qquad \begin{array}{r} 5 \\ \times\ 6 \\ \hline \end{array} \qquad \begin{array}{r} 11 \\ \times\ 6 \\ \hline \end{array} \qquad \begin{array}{r} 6 \\ \times\ 5 \\ \hline \end{array} \qquad \begin{array}{r} 10 \\ \times\ 6 \\ \hline \end{array}$$

$$\begin{array}{r} 1 \\ \times\ 6 \\ \hline \end{array} \qquad \begin{array}{r} 7 \\ \times\ 6 \\ \hline \end{array} \qquad \begin{array}{r} 6 \\ \times\ 9 \\ \hline \end{array} \qquad \begin{array}{r} 6 \\ \times\ 8 \\ \hline \end{array} \qquad \begin{array}{r} 3 \\ \times\ 6 \\ \hline \end{array} \qquad \begin{array}{r} 2 \\ \times\ 6 \\ \hline \end{array}$$

SEVEN TIMES PRACTICE

7 x 1 =

7 x 3 =

7 x 4 =

7 x 2 =

8 x 7 =

5 x 7 =

6 x 7 =

9 x 7 =

MORE PRACTICE...

7 x 1 = ___   5 x 7 = ___   7 x 4 = ___

9 x 7 = ___   7 x 8 = ___   10 x 7 = ___

7 x 3 = ___   2 x 7 = ___   7 x 7 = ___

11 x 7 = ___   7 x 6 = ___   12 x 7 = ___

$$\begin{array}{r} 7 \\ \times\ 1 \\ \hline \end{array} \qquad \begin{array}{r} 7 \\ \times\ 3 \\ \hline \end{array} \qquad \begin{array}{r} 5 \\ \times\ 7 \\ \hline \end{array} \qquad \begin{array}{r} 2 \\ \times\ 7 \\ \hline \end{array} \qquad \begin{array}{r} 7 \\ \times\ 7 \\ \hline \end{array} \qquad \begin{array}{r} 7 \\ \times\ 6 \\ \hline \end{array}$$

$$\begin{array}{r} 11 \\ \times\ 7 \\ \hline \end{array} \qquad \begin{array}{r} 7 \\ \times\ 2 \\ \hline \end{array} \qquad \begin{array}{r} 4 \\ \times\ 7 \\ \hline \end{array} \qquad \begin{array}{r} 10 \\ \times\ 7 \\ \hline \end{array} \qquad \begin{array}{r} 7 \\ \times\ 8 \\ \hline \end{array} \qquad \begin{array}{r} 11 \\ \times\ 7 \\ \hline \end{array}$$

$$\begin{array}{r} 9 \\ \times\ 7 \\ \hline \end{array} \qquad \begin{array}{r} 7 \\ \times\ 7 \\ \hline \end{array} \qquad \begin{array}{r} 7 \\ \times\ 2 \\ \hline \end{array} \qquad \begin{array}{r} 7 \\ \times\ 5 \\ \hline \end{array} \qquad \begin{array}{r} 3 \\ \times\ 7 \\ \hline \end{array} \qquad \begin{array}{r} 4 \\ \times\ 7 \\ \hline \end{array}$$

EIGHT TIMES PRACTICE

8 x 6 =

8 x 7 =

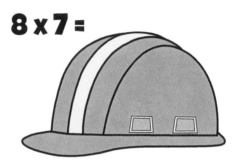

8 x 2 =

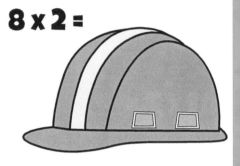

8 x 9 =

8 x 5 =

8 x 1 =

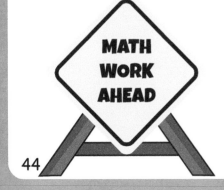

MATH WORK AHEAD

UNDER CONSTRUCTION

MATH WORK AHEAD

44

MORE PRACTICE...

8 x 4 =___   2 x 8 =___   8 x 1 =___

8 x 8 =___   8 x 9 =___   12 x 8 =___

8 x 5 =___   3 x 8 =___   8 x 6 =___

11 x 8 =___   8 x 7 =___   10 x 8 =___

```
    8          8          3          6          8          8
 x  8       x  1       x  8       x  8       x  5       x  6
_____    _____    _____    _____    _____    _____
```

```
   10          8          5         12          8         11
 x  8       x  4       x  8       x  8       x  2       x  8
_____    _____    _____    _____    _____    _____
```

```
    9          1          8          8          3          2
 x  8       x  8       x  9       x  7       x  8       x  8
_____    _____    _____    _____    _____    _____
```

9x NINE TIMES PRACTICE

 9 x 3 =

 9 x 7 =

 9 x 9 =

 9 x 1 =

 9 x 5 =

 4 x 9 =

 2 x 9 =

  6 x 9 =

 7 x 9 =

 3 x 9 =

46

MORE PRACTICE...

9 x 2 =___   4 x 9 =___   9 x 1 =___

8 x 9 =___   9 x 9 =___   10 x 9 =___

9 x 3 =___   5 x 9 =___   9 x 7 =___

12 x 9 =___   9 x 6 =___   11 x 9 =___

```
    9          9          6          3          9          9
  x 1        x 8        x 9        x 9        x 2        x 6
  ___        ___        ___        ___        ___        ___
```

```
   11          9          5         12          9         10
  x 9        x 7        x 9        x 9        x 5        x 9
  ___        ___        ___        ___        ___        ___
```

```
    9          3          9          9          1          7
  x 9        x 9        x 2        x 4        x 9        x 9
  ___        ___        ___        ___        ___        ___
```

10x TEN TIMES PRACTICE

10 x 5 = ___

10 x 7 = ___

10 x 10 = ___

2 x 10 = ___

6 x 10 = ___

3 x 10 = ___

10 x 1 = ___

10 x 7 = ___

10 x 11 = ___

MORE PRACTICE...

10 x 1 = ___   4 x 10 = ___   10 x 3 = ___

7 x 10 = ___   10 x 5 = ___   12 x 10 = ___

10 x 2 = ___   9 x 10 = ___   10 x 6 = ___

10 x 10 = ___   10 x 8 = ___   11 x 10 = ___

10	10	10	10	10	10
x 3	x 5	x 1	x 9	x 2	x 7

10	10	10	10	10	10
x 1	x 2	x 7	x 8	x 5	x 9

10	10	10	10	10	10
x 3	x 8	x 1	x 4	x 6	x 2

11x

 11 x 7 = ◯

 11 x 8 = ◯

 11 x 9 = ◯

ELEVEN TIMES PRACTICE

11 x 2 =

11 x 4 =
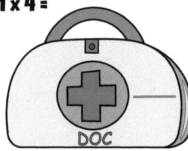

11 x 3 =
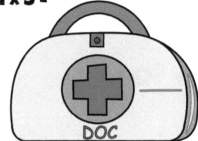

11 x 1 =

11 x 5 =
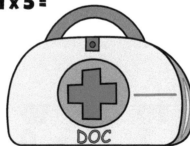

11 x 11 =
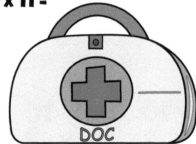

11 x 6 =
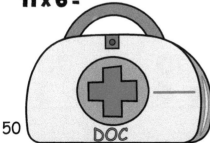

11 x 7 =

11 x 10 =
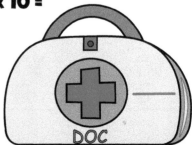

MORE PRACTICE...

11 x 2 = ___   3 x 11 = ___   11 x 1 = ___

8 x 11 = ___   11 x 4 = ___   12 x 11 = ___

11 x 6 = ___   9 x 11 = ___   11 x 5 = ___

11 x 11 = ___   11 x 7 = ___   10 x 11 = ___

```
    11        11        11        11        11        11
  x  1      x  5      x  3      x  8      x  2      x  7
  ____      ____      ____      ____      ____      ____
```

```
    11        11        11        11        11        11
  x  2      x  4      x  7      x  9      x  5      x  6
  ____      ____      ____      ____      ____      ____
```

```
    11        11        11        11        11        11
  x  3      x  4      x  6      x  1      x  4      x  2
  ____      ____      ____      ____      ____      ____
```

51

TWELVE TIMES PRACTICE

12x

12 x 1 = _____

12 x 3 = _____

12 x 5 = _____

12 x 9 = _____

12 x 11 = _____

12 X 2 = __

12 X 4 = __

12 X 6 = __

12 X 8 = __

52

MORE PRACTICE...

12 x 1 = __   4 x 12 = __   12 x 2 = __

9 x 12 = __   12 x 3 = __   12 x 12 = __

12 x 7 = __   8 x 12 = __   12 x 5 = __

11 x 12 = __   12 x 6 = __   10 x 12 = __

12	12	12	12	12	12
x 3	x 8	x 1	x 5	x 2	x 6

12	12	12	12	12	12
x 2	x 3	x 9	x 7	x 5	x 7

12	12	12	12	12	12
x 7	x 4	x 6	x 4	x 1	x 2

MULTIPLICATION TABLE

FILL IN THE MULTIPLICATION TABLE!

1
Track your finger down the yellow column of numbers on the left side of the table until you find the first number in a question.

2
Now, track a different finger along the blue row of numbers at the top of the table until it matches the second number in a question.

3
Finally, run your first finger across the table and your second finger down the table. The number where your fingers meet is where you write your answer.

X	1	2	3	4	5	6	7	8	9	10	11	12
1												
2												
3												
4												
5												
6												
7												
8												
9												
10												
11												
12												

54

FOR MORE
TIMES TABLE TRICKS

WWW.LARISSABJORNSON.com

CPSIA information can be obtained
at www.ICGtesting.com
Printed in the USA
BVHW022024140621
609534BV00011B/1852